Is It Dusk or Is It Dawn

A Hopeful Journey through Grief

❦

Corinne Elizabeth Van Meter

Dedication

For all our loved ones who have made the journey on...

Table of Contents

Foreward

We have heard that life is eternal. Yet, when we lose a loved one in death, we are shaken to the core of our being and so often we question our beliefs. It is right to question, for through that process we can eventually be led to an even deeper understanding.

Corinne is a mother who shares her journey of how her daughter communicated with her after she left her physical body. As a mother who has lost one child at birth and a second in a car accident, I know personally of *their* connections beyond this body temple. In my work, I've also had the opportunity to assist many others in finding those new bonds after the loss of a beloved.

Discover with Corinne the joy of realizing there is more to life than meets the eye. See how you, too, can listen with your heart and hear from a loved one on the 'other side' of life.

Rev. Elizabeth Forrest
Unity Church of Winston-Salem
Winston-Salem, NC

Acknowledgements

I had a wonderful childhood because of my parents, John Paul and Betty Louise Loboda, who created a space of love to start me out on the journey here. I always knew I was loved and respected, and I still feel that, even though you have both moved on. Mother, your open mind nurtured my soul and helped me see so many things. You made it easier for me to grow into who I am. The example of your life will always be my inspiration… thank you.

Thank you, Vicki, and all those spirits that speak with me. When you talk, I promise I'll do my best to listen!

And thanks be to God, the Creator, the Source of all that is seen and unseen!

Just when the caterpillar thought

the world was over,

it became a butterfly.

—Proverb

Introduction

August 2008

Less than five months ago, I lost my daughter. I say lost, but I know exactly where she is. Events since that moment of pain have pointed the way for me to find her. I now have a deeper understanding not only of life but also of "death," that experience that lies on the other side of the thin veil covering this reality that you and I are now choosing to live. I know that place exists; my daughter has helped me see it very clearly for she communicates to me from where she now resides. If that kind of communication can happen to me, it can happen to you, too…it *does* happen to you. You just don't allow yourself to believe it yet. Let me help you believe.

I feel I have both a personal need and a spiritual calling to share my experience with you. All I can do is tell you my story. How you accept it and what you do with it is then your choice. I hope that my words will float into your heart and whisper to your spirit because *your truth*, indeed, can set you free!

Birds sing, hearts hear,

love circles, life roars!

—Corinne Van Meter

Isn't Life Great?

Early March 2008

I think it was on a hike at Bryce Canyon in Utah when my husband turned to me in the grandeur of the red rock and said, "If everything ended right here and now, if life was over for us in this instant, we've had more fabulous experiences in this lifetime than we could have ever imagined!" I am certain that I returned the sentiment. That exchange had taken place countless times in myriad places all over the world, from the thermal spas of Iceland to the Great Wall of China, from the splendor of the Canadian Rockies to the rainforests of Central America. Yes, indeed, our lives were filled with so many spectacular and exciting moments.

Jim and I had been married for almost thirty-nine years. Those years brought some challenging junctures to us, but we managed to help each other through those times with understanding and with an underlying freedom that we both, in our own ways, granted each other. I had met twenty-seven-year-old Jim at the tender age of seventeen and was married to him shortly after my high school graduation. While I got my teaching degree, my husband developed a campground business and then eventually trained to become a stockbroker, a job that he held for the majority of his working life. I had taught school for a couple of years, and when we started our family, I traded in my teacher training to be an at-home mom to our three children. After twenty-two years of actively participating in the lives of my children, I chose to return to the classroom, working with at-risk youth in a different state. My life had been so rewarding and rich; I would not have changed a moment. My adventurous and generous husband had provided me with so many opportunities and encouraged me to grow in unexpected ways. We both did that for each other.

We also shared that freedom with our children—the freedom to imagine, to dream, to be, and to experience. I think it started with all those trips to Disney World, our family's favorite vacation spot. What a place to dream! We knew every nook and cranny it seemed! I'm embarrassed to say just how many trips we made there. But each wonderful trip was worth it. There was Thanksgiving at Epcot, a birthday at Cinderella's Castle, and breakfast with Mickey, as well as so many other precious times together. We were blessed to be able to do it all, but many of those times, we sacrificed to make it happen. I am so glad that we took every trip. Memories are what you have when everything else goes away.

We were always a bit unconventional in our lifestyle choices, a blend of conservative thought mixed with a liberal dose of serendipity thrown in. We prided ourselves with going to great lengths to expose our children, who were now grown, to people, places and limitless ideas all through their lives. Whatever they had an interest in, we encouraged them to try. Sports. Arts. Music. Travel. Camps. Pets. The bookstore was another favorite family place. We could always spend hours there! It seemed to have worked out. What a fascinating mix of individuals we nurtured! Each one possesses a different brand of courage, and each one has a unique identity. All were compassionate and caring and had genuinely good souls. Of that, we were the most proud.

Elizabeth, our oldest, was born with so much creative talent. She could dance and sing, she was an artist as well as a basketball player, and she could act! She excelled in the arts from an early age and seemed destined for a career in the theater, so we did what we could to help create that opportunity for her. Using her skills, she had earned her way into a prestigious arts school as a high school senior and then continued to work at perfecting her skills attending college there as she studied for her BA in Fine Arts. Now she is following her lifelong dream by pursuing her career in New York City. We have been there to see her in a number of shining performances. We have watched her in movies, have seen her on the stage, heard her voice work, and spotted her picture on billboards. She is still working hard at making her mark. We are so proud of her and all her accomplishments.

Daniel, our son, the traveler, interrupted his college education to serve in the U.S. Army, feeling that he needed more discipline, and found himself in Iraq only six months after signing up. He completed two tours of duty, becoming a sergeant and then traveled by himself across the United States after his discharge. He had dreamed of doing that when he was in Iraq, and his trip of a lifetime almost turned into a lifetime trip, but now he has settled into New York City where he is finally completing his college education. He wants to become a high school history teacher, and what a fine one he will make.

And then there is Vicki, the light of all of our lives from the moment she was born. Vicki, her laughter, her smile always lights up our whole family. What a life she has led thus far! So intelligent, so adventurous, with a rebel nature that always pushes the envelope! We enjoy her spirit. That spirit allowed her to do some remarkable things at an early age. She took flying lessons at the age of ten and ended up flying a single-engine plane across America at eleven. The year after that, she piloted a single-engine plane across the Atlantic Ocean. She flew with an instructor in the plane, but each time, *she* did the legwork and the flying.

Unbelievable! She has been on television, has given speeches at almost all the NASA centers across the country, and has even been invited to the White House. I could go on and on, but right now, those events don't seem to matter so much. Oh, the adventures she has led us on…we, her parents, were there for them all. Years after those exciting events, we have even gone to the country of Moldova to visit her when she, after earning a degree in criminal justice, joined the United States Peace Corps and was assigned there. Vicki is still accomplishing things, but she has some personal issues she is working on. For many years, our spirited daughter fought that enemy called depression. We had all tried to help her at different times and in various ways throughout the years, but with her independent nature, she pushed us away from those dark places, and she grew to keep them secret from us, dealing with her problems in her own way. But still, knowing her realistic view of life and her strength, we had faith that she was meeting her challenges and would overcome her battles. She is moving forward, or so we thought, maybe hoped. She returned from Peace Corps service recently and has taken a job as a surveillance investigator working long, strange hours in difficult circumstances, but it is so like Vicki to push herself into doing something tough like that. So like Vicki.

So much promise, so much possibility for all of them, all of our children. We were in awe of our lives. Both of us were retired—Jim hiking out west, me dabbling in writing and making jewelry back east. Both of us were healthy, and both of us were satisfied. The most important part of our lives is our children, each one so interesting, each one so challenging. There was always something exciting on our journey with them. No one was married yet, and we obviously didn't have any grandchildren. We could wait on all of that. We just wanted our children to be happy, that's all. Yes, there were some bumps on the road, but everyone has those and time has a way of taking care of things. Not everything was perfect, but pretty darned close. We were blessed. Wasn't life great?

Rain falls and still the birds sing...

—Corinne Van Meter

No

Palm Sunday. I was in church, a place that always brought me a feeling of great joy. They had asked for volunteers to sing the next week on Easter Sunday and had called for a practice right after this Sunday's service. After a visit to the church bookstore to purchase the minister-recommended book, *The Week That Changed the World*, I took my place with the choir and sang my heart out. In fact, as I sang "I Have a Dream", a song that would be sung on Peace Sunday, my voice sounded to me especially clear and I felt the meaning of the words and the vibration of the sounds in my heart.

I rushed home and reminded myself to make the second call that day to my daughter, Vicki. It was her father's birthday, and she had made me promise to remind her of it so that she would call him. She had to start back to work that afternoon after missing a month because she had broken a bone in her ankle. Actually, a few days before the break, she had gotten into an accident on the way to a surveillance job early one snowy, icy morning and had totaled the company van. Nothing like that had ever happened to her before, and the loss of control that she felt while sliding across the highway and hitting a guard rail seemed to have really shaken our fearless daughter. She had taken it easy for a number of weeks, watching movies on the sofa of our family's home in Pennsylvania and letting her ankle heal. I was in North Carolina writing, and Jim was in Utah hiking. She appreciated her privacy. Vicki loved to watch movies from her giant collection. She also liked cooking a "feast" to eat, truly an event for her as it wasn't so long ago that she was living in a foreign country where eating was, well, not quite like home. She had communicated on the phone quite normally with some of her friends during this time.

But, it was time to go out on a job again, and she told me that she had so many things to do in preparation that she didn't want to forget to call her dad on his birthday. I had called her once already, and she hadn't answered. This was the second time this day. That was not unusual because she sometimes, for her own reasons, ignored our calls. I would usually text her and say that we'd have to call the neighbors and have them come over and check on her, and then she'd call back real fast to avoid that embarrassing situation. But I hadn't heard anything from her, so I became concerned.

I had also tried to reach her the night before, several times with no response. We shared the same birthday, which was just three days earlier. We had called each other many times, of course. We sort of joked back and forth all day singing, "Happy Birthday. Happy Birthday." I had bought a number of gifts and wrapped them and sent them to her in a big box with instructions *not* to open them until her birthday. This was her first birthday in the United States since Peace Corps, and I knew it was an important one to honor. She waited until after midnight and had a personal birthday. I had hoped she would be pleased with my selections and with the surprises I sent, even gifts from her two dogs, both of which I was watching for her as her job took her away for days at a time. Her father had sent her some flowers, too. She was so happy with everything. In fact, despite the accident and the broken bone, she had been happy this last month. We were back and forth on the phone, laughing over *American Idol* and *Little People, Big World*. She had found the time during her recovery to finally apply to graduate school and had put the finishing touches on what I thought was a great application. I had been her proofreader. We all toasted the future even at a distance.

On Saturday, the day before this day, I received some flowers from her, something that had never before happened. Actually, it was sort of a "thing" that *my* birthday wasn't a big deal every year, but *her* birthday needed to be. She loved extending her birthday for days, and we tried to do that, so it was sweet of her to send me flowers a couple days after my birthday. I called her to thank her. No answer. In fact, I called her four times and texted her, with no response, but I figured she was getting ready for the trip she had to take. There was so much to be done. But now, having received no response from her for the second day, I was concerned.

I called Jim, in Utah, and told him. Even though we can find ourselves miles apart, we are always in constant contact. He called one of her neighbors, who said he had seen and talked with Vicki the day before, and he reassured Jim that she must be preparing for her trip or maybe she overslept. He confirmed that she was busy working to get everything ready to leave later that afternoon. Vicki took her job seriously and would have gotten on the road and called us en route if she thought she would be late. Still, Jim asked her neighbor to use the key that we had given him for the house and to please check on Vicki.

After speaking with my husband, I busied myself around the house, anxiously awaiting a return call confirming Vicki's whereabouts. I had no reason to be alarmed, but I was reasonably concerned. Finally, I received the call that changed my life, the call that changed my world. In a frantic, breathless voice, Jim gasped in my ear, "Vicki shot herself!" My heart stood still, and all I could do was woefully scream, "Noooo!" as my body melted.

How I composed myself, I do not know. I believe that we are touched by God's grace at moments like these in our lives giving us unbelievable strength. "How could this possibly be?" I asked in my struggle to understand. "What should I do?" my mind shouted as I grasped for something to hold on to. Jim was in Utah trying to get the details and make arrangements for us to get home; Elizabeth and Daniel were in New York City; I was in North Carolina, and Vicki, in Pennsylvania.

I waited to hear more news from Jim. Something deep inside told me that she was gone, but my heart and mind couldn't believe that it was true. *How could it be?* I had just talked with her on Friday. She was preparing for her first day back to work. Yes, she was frustrated, but *how could this be?* I just got flowers from her in the mail yesterday and a balloon and a funny birthday message. *What? How could this have happened? What should I do?* Annie, I'll call my friend, Annie. She'll come over. Then, I called my minister and my sister and sister-in-law who live in still another state. My children…Vicki, my beautiful daughter…my heart…I could feel it pounding in my chest. I had felt Vicki drifting away from me in recent months, the cord that connected us stretching, taking us farther and farther apart, but now it was cut, and I felt myself all alone floating in a sea of pain. *Breathe, Corinne, breathe!* I closed my eyes as tears streamed down my face, and I sank into the floor hugging my heart. All we were left with was a note with her last words, words that she wrote and left on the kitchen counter—"Take comfort in knowing there was nothing anyone could have said or done to prevent this from happening"—words that we would have to grow to understand.

I share this painful part of my life with you to let you know that I understand your pain. Loss, all loss, is the same: the pain, the aching emptiness, the space inside full of unending hurt. Anytime we lose someone we love, the cry that our heart makes is so loud. I hear your cries. I hear your heart. I embrace you, and I want to help you. I am in hopes that you will find in the following pages some inspiration for relieving the suffering that has come into your life at this time. Maybe your loss has come now, perhaps it will enter your life sometime in the future, but at this moment, I want to show you an opportunity that faces you—an opportunity to see life in a new way. I offer you a chance to react differently to your loss and to expand your world in ways that you may never have known. I share with you our family's journey after the tragic loss of one so very loved.

It's so hard to say good-bye, to close the door and wonder why...It has to be that we must part, for now you must live in my heart.

—Corinne Van Meter

Listening with New Ears

Our kind neighbors had handled all the horrible aftermath of the tragedy at our home, and we were so grateful to them. We did not have to live through the shock of finding her. What faced us would be difficult enough. Jim and Elizabeth flew to North Carolina, and a family friend, thank God for him, drove us the seven hours from North Carolina to Pittsburgh, where we met Daniel at the airport. Then we drove the long, painful drive to our hometown where we would see Vicki as we had never before seen her. The agonizing ride back was full of tears, shock, and total disbelief.

We began sharing our last conversations with Vicki trying to make some sense of it all, not understanding much. Jim had revealed that earlier in the week he and Vicki had a kind of joking conversation in which the subject of cremation came up. The topic was not brought up by Vicki. Jim's uncle had died a few years back, and Jim, the only living relative, had yet to find a resting spot for his uncle's ashes. They had a discussion about it and both had shared what they would want to have done to themselves if something happened to either one of them. Vicki had said she definitely wanted to be cremated when she died and continued on to share where she wanted her ashes to rest. Unbelievable as it may seem, Jim's innocent conversation with his daughter let us know what to do in the wake of this tragedy. Vicki had prepared us with her words. At least we had some direction, and by following it, we would be respecting her wishes.

Cremation was planned for the next day, so the moments we had with her the evening we arrived would be some of our last. As we entered the strange new world of the funeral home, Elizabeth and I lagged behind. We wanted to remember Vicki as she had been. Jim and Daniel immediately disappeared down the hall to the room where she had been taken after being prepared for us to see. Jim quickly bolted through the door back to us and reassuringly pleaded that we *had* to come in to see her, we just *had* to. So, Elizabeth and I hesitantly followed him as he led us down the corridor toward the room where Vicki lay.

What we saw was an incredible vision. Wrapped in a plain, white sheet, my daughter seemed to lie as a goddess before us surrounded by a radiance not of this earth. Her perfect face reflected a deep, true beauty that glowed with peace and serenity. We were astonished and soon began realizing that *we could actually feel her presence in the room!* It was unmistakable! It was as if Vicki was finally revealing her true self to us. Something powerful touched my soul and helped me stand amid the despair. My tears stopped, and I suddenly understood how holy this moment really was. I heard myself murmur to her beautiful, luminescent physical body, "It was a privilege to be your mother," while knowing that her essence could hear our every word. We all stood in awe and prayed aloud to her from our open hearts, asking her to help us get through this torment. How could we face the rest of our lives without her? We stood around her, pleading for her to help us. I am so grateful for having those moments with her. My mind's eye will remember each detail, and my heart will never forget.

I am not so strong that I do not weep.

I am not so weak that I cannot stand.

—Corinne Van Meter

Opening Up

I believe that our journey of recognizing and receiving Vicki's presence in our lives began during those moments when we were all together with her in that room at the funeral home. *We actually felt Vicki's amazing spirit present in the room all around us, and we felt her peace.* We asked for her help in facing this terrible loss, and from that night on, we were connected with that part of her that has been, is, and always will be. Her beautiful spirit came to us, sometimes through thoughts, even through touch. Being open to receiving her allowed us to follow our intuitions, and in so doing, Vicki's spirit had a chance to speak with us, each one of us hearing just what we needed to know. With Vicki's help and guidance, we began moving in the direction of deeper understanding. We were able to make the necessary decisions involving what we should do for her, and many important decisions needed to be made.

The first decision was that of having our own private service for Vicki. She had been in the public eye and was known by many because of her accomplishments. We knew Vicki as a humble, unpretentious, private person, and we decided to have a time just for us and for her. We didn't even include extended family members just yet—a family which is composed of many aunts, uncles, and cousins, not to mention dear friends and caring souls close to us all. It became a time for us to connect with Vicki and for us to heal in moments between us as a family without any outside interference from well-meaning people. We focused all our attention and energy on connecting to our bond with each other and with Vicki. It made our decisions so much easier because it caused us to use all our energy in a positive way, no unnecessary scattering of emotions. This time, immediately after "death," is so very precious. The light, the spirit transitioning from the body, is still close. It is a time for connection, for feeling the light, and that was what we were trying to do. In our case, we were desperately trying to understand Vicki, and she obviously was doing all in her power to contact us, to reassure us, and to help us understand. We were in constant awareness of her, had no distractions, and were in a clear place despite our sadness. This allowed us the ability to recognize Vicki's spirit speaking to us.

May I add that we were raised up, lifted to a higher level of consciousness, if you will, by prayers and healing thoughts from our relatives, friends, and so many people all over the country, even the world, for the account of Vicki's passing was spreading over this planet. All that positive energy was directed toward us and helped to make miracles happen. I am forever grateful to all those compassionate souls who responded with love, for that love cradled our hearts, brought us comfort, and made all the difference. This had also happened during Vicki's flights many years ago. Jim and I had felt the power of prayer then, too. The prayers of many carried our daughter safely home then, and now prayers were raising her family to be healed as she embarked on a new journey. How important it is to hold in our hearts others who are grieving. This experience made us appreciate more deeply others' pain. How different it would be for us from now on.

Newspaper reporters were calling. They were eager to contact us and learn details about what had happened. We had to decide how to respond to them. We felt guided by Vicki and knew that she would want us to speak the truth, so we did just that, making public her struggle with depression. Just weeks prior to this day, Vicki had written her essay to a graduate school in which she discussed her reasons for desiring to obtain a master's in psychology. She had wanted to work with youth and as she put it "remove the stigma of seeking help" for mental conditions.

Vicki had been through an emotionally challenging adolescence, and as an adult, she was working through her own resulting issues, relying on no one but herself. She could not accept help. She was highly intelligent and believed that she should be able to cope. It was a struggle each day, and we didn't realize just how difficult it had been for her. We knew she was hurting, but she chose to hide so much from us. She had battled valiantly, but had lost on that one night a few days earlier. As much as she kept from us, we were now in a place of deeply connecting with her and knew that she was telling us to help her make a difference now, even if she wasn't in the world to see it through. So, we listened to our inner voices and calmly responded as we felt Vicki would want us. She had been an inspiration in her coming with her early achievements in flying, and in her going, she would be a different kind of an inspiration, shedding light on depression. We just *knew* those were her desires.

Talk to me.

—Vicki Van Meter

Messages

We did not think that any of us would sleep that first night, but something very unusual happened to each one of us. In fact, we slept so soundly that unbeknownst to us, our neighbor had slipped quietly inside our living room placing a single rose on the table to represent all the people who cared about Vicki outside of her immediate family. He wanted her to know that many others were with her in spirit. The rose would be included in the cremation ceremony the next day. In what we would have expected to be an excruciating night, it was as if we had been sprinkled with angel dust, because miraculously, we slept though to morning light from that night on. And during those hours of sleep, some of us heard Vicki's voice, saw her, and even felt her touch.

Both Elizabeth and Daniel spent the following week or so with us in sort of a retreat time. Neighbors and friends brought food for us, and aside from some close friends and limited family visits, we just stayed in the house together, being present with each other and with Vicki. Night can be the hardest time to get through, but for us, it became a time of anticipation as Vicki came to us, especially then. And each morning brought the sharing of the events of the night before. *There was no doubt that we were experiencing contact with Vicki's amazing spirit!* She seemed to know what pain we were in, what pain her decision had brought us, and she was desperately trying to help us understand. We came to depend on her help and by being open to her, by really listening, and by honoring what we were experiencing, we were *allowing* her to help us, and ended up by helping ourselves. She continues to do that for us to this day, and we continue to be open to her help.

After the first night, Daniel received messages from Vicki as he meditated upon waking. He described what he was receiving as thoughts in his head that seemed to come from her, thoughts that brought him understanding. Translating those thoughts into words was difficult for him. Words are human. How does one translate thoughts of understanding? He tried to use words that he thought we would understand when explaining what had been revealed to him. Everything he told us made sense and seemed to be meant to bring us peace and comfort. He told us that she didn't care what anyone else thought, only what we, her family thought. That sounded like something Vicki would say, as did the other messages that Daniel related to us. He told us that she believed that we could handle this—she chose to be with us for a reason, adding that she never intended to be here on the earth for a long time. She reminded him that we were missing part of the whole story and that we would try to understand, but that we couldn't because we didn't have all the parts. She knew that we were thinking that if we could have shown her more love or done something different, we could have prevented what happened, but she wanted us to know that *there is so much more to it than that and that we couldn't see these factors because we were in the physical world.* She told him that *this doesn't have to be hard* and that there was work for her to do someplace else. She also said something else that changed how we thought: *if you are sad, you'll be thinking of yourself. When you are happy, you'll be thinking of me.* But one of her messages helped us to open even more: *talk to me.*

When you hear things, or shall I say hear thoughts, it can be somewhat difficult at first to conceive that they might actually be coming from a source other than imagination. Our earthly being naturally questions such happenings. It seems impossible to believe what we are hearing. But acknowledging that we were receiving real messages made our connection with Vicki only strengthen. We quickly embraced those thoughts, and they continued to come to us. We did talk to her, and we definitely heard her answer back!

One night, Elizabeth crawled into bed next to me as she was feeling alone and wanted the comfort of someone close by. As I lay there with thoughts of Vicki in my heart, I began to feel a gentle touch that traveled from the top of my head to my forehead. Then a gentle smile made its way to my mouth. I felt sort of paralyzed; I could not speak and could do nothing more than remain in this feeling of suspension, my mouth fixed in a peaceful smile. Eventually, I lapsed into slumber and awoke the next day with a faint memory of the night's events. Later on in the afternoon, Elizabeth and I were talking about the previous night, and she told me of something that happened to her. She began to relate a story of being touched on the top of her head and of having a smile on her face that wouldn't stop, and then she had fallen asleep. At the same moments I had experienced the touch and the smile, Elizabeth felt the very same feelings. We were both sure that it was Vicki helping us to find some peace that night. One of her signatures in this life was a smile that came from the warmth of her very soul, a smile that could make anyone smile.

Out of all of us, Jim was struggling the most, but it was he that quickly began having nightly conversations with Vicki. She would come to him as he slept and talk with him, answer his questions, and then he would wake up afterward and look at the clock. It would usually happen between three and five in the morning. She eventually ended up explaining the events that led up to her leaving, her frame of mind, and her choice. She told him, *"Dad, I needed help and I wouldn't allow myself to get help on earth, but now I have all the help I need. I'm all right."* Only once did he question her on the brutal choice that she made, asking, "How could you have done this?" and the answer came right back loud and clear: *"Don't give that a second thought, Dad; it was just the quickest way to get here."* She kept coming to him in dreamtime for weeks in conversations, in happenings that he could sometimes not remember, yet he knew he had been comforted by her presence. Once she had told him, *"Dad, I see everything in a different light now, which I couldn't see at all while I was on earth, but it goes both ways. You can see me in an entirely different light now that I'm not on earth."* One night before going to sleep, he asked her if he could see her, and that night he saw her in a dream. *He saw her.* She was smiling and looked beautiful in a dress. Vicki didn't wear many dresses on earth, but

I suppose she wanted her father to see her in one. He was exuberantly happy, and of course, shared that with us, and you can imagine the peace and joy it brought him.

One evening as Jim slept, Vicki told him, *"When you hear a bird chirping or see a rainbow, think of me."* He shared it with me the next day. Funny, I reminded him, hadn't we been hearing woodpeckers each morning during the weeks since Vicki's leaving? I recalled that after Vicki had done her flying and was giving talks at NASA all around the country, she had a part in her speech where she told a favorite story about the woodpecker. The point of the story was that all the woodpecker could do was peck; he couldn't sing like the other birds. So, instead of concentrating on what he couldn't do, he chose to do what he could do with all his might! It sure felt like Vicki was showing us what she could now do!

On the third day after Vicki left, I heard the words, *"No more tears."* Vicki was always accusing me of being too emotional and would get embarrassed when I'd cry in public or at home, for that matter. Well, from that day on, for the most part, I have held onto that message because somewhere inside, I understood. Something came over me and allowed me to go to that place of calm and peace. I believe Vicki, or that which is God—all the wisdom of the universe, helped me there. A feeling of profound understanding became a part of me, and I was able to help those around me by saying things that I just seemed to instinctively know. Once again, I was filled with God's grace. Of course, Vicki's messages came through in thoughts all the time, day and night. She kept telling me, *"I'm here, Mother; I'm here in your heart!"* I knew it was her. She never called me Mom; it was always Mother.

I remember standing in line at the store thinking of her when I noticed the music that was playing in the background. The words of the song were an answer to my thoughts. One night I know I was "flying" with her in my dreams, and once when I woke up around 5:00 a.m., I smelled the fragrance of flowers gently wafting through the air. Another night, I had a dream that I saw Vicki on the green banks of a peaceful, flowing river. She said to me, *"I am the river; I am you...all of life is connected. It is God in all."* I continued to have these messages come to me with clarity. I was afraid to write any of them down because I couldn't quite put them into words. There were no words, only feelings. I just knew that Vicki was with me, helping me see more than I had ever seen before. I did try to maintain a small journal so I could remind myself of these profound moments—so that I could relive my divine connection to my daughter.

There were so many stories of those connections for us. I can't begin to address them all, but one stands out during the time when we took Elizabeth and Daniel back to New York City, where we experienced a very special message. We had just accompanied Elizabeth downtown so she could check in at her workplace, and Jim and I passed the time waiting for her at a bookstore. We slowly and sort of aimlessly wandered around the store, picked up a few things for purchase, and found ourselves in the long line at the checkout. I looked around and something caught my eye on the carousel before me. Right at eye level, just a couple feet away, was a small book. Let me explain something. When Vicki was just two, her imaginative and dramatic nine-year-old sister, Elizabeth, had managed to convince her that she was a pig. Vicki believed it and introduced herself to people as Vicki Toria, the pig. She had kept the identity until her father took her to the fair several years later to catch a glimpse of the "World's Largest Pig." She changed her mind about things after that but always had a soft spot for pig memorabilia. Vicki was known for her sense of humor and was dubbed Hammy by the family, and everyone who knew her could call her by that endearing name. The book before my eyes was called *The Pig of Happiness!* I picked it up and began reading it along with my husband. *The words of this unusual little book spoke Vicki's story!* Right there in my hand was a message from our daughter—a way for her to reach us and let us know that she was indeed happy. Was the man who wrote this quirky little book that meant so much to us, perhaps part of our lives? Somehow, we are all connected to each other, entwined in ways that we cannot know. I immediately got a book for each one of us, and as we read them together around the table at dinner, Vicki spoke to us in our hearts and our eyes welled with tears.

There was another message that came to us in a book shortly after Vicki's passing. Actually, it was a message for my husband. He had been in his den looking at pictures of Vicki that he had collected over the years when he found, hidden among the shelves, a wrapped package that he had placed there years ago. He pulled it out and noticed the writing. It was addressed: 'To: Vicki, From: Dad'.

He remembered that he had purchased it for her some time ago. Vicki was not in a good place emotionally then, and it had caused some trying times in their relationship. Jim had feared that if something happened to him, Vicki might be filled with guilt, and he wanted to spare her heart from suffering. Jim and I were on a trip across the country, and in a small town somewhere in Virginia, we had stopped at a lovely little bookstore where he had discovered the beautiful book of illustrations of a poem titled *My Wish for You.* Jim had purchased it and then had it gift wrapped, and after we returned home, he addressed it to Vicki and hid it on the shelf in his den. He had thought that if something ever happened to him, she would eventually find it. *Now it was here for him!* Vicki had helped him find it on the day that he needed it. We both read it together with tear-stained faces and knew that the book was not his gift to Vicki, but her gift to her father. The poem read:

This Is My Wish for You...

That the spirit of beauty may continually hover about you and
hold you close within the tenderness of her wings.
That each beautiful and gracious thing in life
may be unto you a symbol of good
for your soul's delight.
That sun-glories and star-glories,
Leaf-glories and bark-glories,

Flower-glories and glories
that lurk in the grasses of the field...
Glories of mountains and oceans,
of little streams of running waters
Glories of song
of posey,
of all the arts...
May be to you as sweet,
abiding influences
That will illumine your life
and make you glad.
That your soul may be
as an alabaster cup,
Filled to overflowing
With the mystical wine
of beauty and love.
That happiness may
put her arms around you,
And wisdom make
your soul serene.
This is my wish for you.

by Charles Livingston Snell (1914)

So many moments of recognizing her presence surrounded us during those trying first days. During that time, I know that I had the distinct feeling of having hands touch the crown of my head almost constantly. If we hadn't been open to hearing Vicki's new voice—a voice that can come in unexpected ways and at unexpected moments, a voice that can be felt through the senses—those precious moments could have been lost to us, and we would have blocked the peace that she was trying to bring us. Imagine what it must be like on the other side trying to communicate with your family on earth. They attempt to reach us, even coming to us in our dreams when our bodies are at rest and our spirits are free. We may not remember these visits. Imagine, if you will, two adjoining hotel rooms, each one having a door that can be opened to the next connecting room. If a person in one room opens his door and the person in the other room keeps his door locked, the two parties will never connect. Entry into the next room depends on *both* sides unlocking and opening their door. I believe this is the situation for those in the next world. Their door is unlocked, and they are totally aware of our room. When we willingly move through our grief, disbelief, and fear, we can open our door and let our loved one enter our world. *When we consciously allow ourselves to do that, such wonder awaits us!*

*I find it easier to recognize her presence
than to dwell on her absence.*

—Corinne Van Meter

How Are You Getting through This?

During this time of adjustment to our new life without the physical presence of Vicki, people, including my own family, began noticing that I was handling it—in their words—well, and it seemed to surprise them. Maybe it looked that way because I appeared to be in a state of calm. Again, for some reason, I was filled with a deep sense of knowing almost from the start as if I had been in some way prepared for this trial. I do not know. I do know that we were each in various places with our acceptance of the tragedy that had come into our lives. When something so horrible, so devastating happens, and losses like this occur every single day to so many of us, when they do enter our lives, we can feel as if we have been slammed into a brick wall. We are stunned, broken, and we question our beliefs. In order for me to go on existing, I had to force myself to stand up, shake myself off, and ask, "Corinne, what do you *truly* believe?" To answer that question, I had to reach into the deepest part of my soul and connect with myself in a more profound way. It became my opportunity to journey farther than I had ever gone before.

Easter came the Sunday after my daughter chose to leave this plane. I had sung the glorious message *"Jesus Christ is risen, today! Alleluia!"* many times in my fifty-seven years. For the first time in my life, I think that as I stayed in my home mourning the "death" of my daughter on this Easter Sunday, I finally truly understood what the Resurrection meant. I lost my father when I was twenty-two, and my beloved mother left almost eight years ago. My understanding grew with each loss in my life, but it took my daughter's loss now to make the truth come alive in my being. He is risen! He is risen, indeed! *Life does not end!* It continues! The energy of spirit cannot be destroyed! It lives!

One of my favorite prayers from the time I was a little girl was the prayer of St. Francis of Assisi. As an adult, I have always called upon those words in moments of contemplation.

The Prayer of St. Francis

Lord, make me an instrument of your peace;
where there is hatred, let me sow love;
where there is injury, pardon;
where there is doubt, faith;
where there is despair, hope
where there is darkness, light
where there is sadness, joy
O divine Master,
grant that I may not so much seek to be consoled as to console;
to be understood, as to understand;
to be loved, as to love;
for it is in giving that we receive,
it is in pardoning that we are pardoned,
and it is in dying that we are born to Eternal Life.
Amen

"…and it is in dying that we are born to eternal life." Life truly does not end! It continues on throughout all eternity! Now, at this crossroad in my life, I had to find my real truth. *Corinne, if you truly believe these things, then trust in that knowledge and live that belief. Truly live your belief now-at this moment! Make the light of your truth live in your life!* The truth spoke to my heart, and so from those moments on, I truly believed and have demonstrated that belief by embracing the continued life of my daughter, acknowledging her presence in the movements of this earthly life that I am currently living.

At the same time as my heart was blossoming with a fresh awareness of life, I was having dreams and messages that revealed knowledge to me almost nightly. I don't know how to explain it. Doors in my mind were opening, and I was allowed to walk into a new understanding of everything. This took place a lot at night as I slept. It also continued during the day as I read books and as I actively lived in the present moment, observing life around me. I revisited one of my favorite Bible passages as a child. During those days, we were encouraged at public school to start our days with a class Bible reading and a prayer. Every time it was my turn to read before the class, I chose the same passage:

Ecclesiastes, 3:1–9

To everything there is a season and a time to every purpose under heaven:
A time to be born, and a time to die; a time to plant, and a time to pluck up that which is planted;
A time to kill, and a time to heal; a time to break down, and a time to build up;
A time to weep, and a time to laugh; a time to mourn, and a time to dance;
A time to cast away stones, and a time to gather stones together; a time to embrace, and a time to refrain from embracing;
A time to get, and a time to lose; a time to keep, and a time to cast away;
A time to rend, and a time to sew; a time to keep silence, and a time to speak;
A time to love, and a time to hate; a time of war, and a time of peace.

The verses of that chapter have always had meaning for me. Even as a child, it seemed my eyes were open to understanding that all events in life have purpose and that accepting *what is* was part of being happy in this earthly life. There had to be a divine reason for everything. I also reminded myself of something that I had written just a month before our seemingly perfect world changed and we lost Vicki—that *imperfection embraced is perfect peace.* I was feeling a peace amid the storm. Was this the *"peace that passeth all understanding"*? I felt like truth was being revealed to me.

Even my family found it difficult at times to accept my peace and understanding after what had happened in our lives. Sometimes it became frustrating for me as well, but I understood that we were dealing with this life-altering event in different ways and that is as it should be. It was challenging for us to be patient enough to embrace each other's feelings when they were so complex. Along with different life experiences, we each shared separate stories of our own personal relationship with Vicki, and we needed to work through our loss in our own way. But, we also had to get through it together as a family unit. I believe that with Vicki's help, we began communicating with each other at a deeper level, listening and respecting each other's feelings more than we ever had before. Our family relationship was improving, and we were coming even closer together. I tried to explain my feelings by saying, "*I find it easier to recognize her presence, than to dwell on her absence.*" They seemed to understand what I meant, and gradually, with each passing day, we found renewed life in the messages that Vicki continued to send to us. We had asked for her help, and we were receiving it through her new language—the language of light. The light of her love was touching our hearts and our minds and was changing us.

I would be telling an untruth if I did not admit that I have moments when I falter, when my motherly tears flow and when I feel claustrophobic imagining the rest of my life here on earth without her. Somewhere inside of me, I still cannot believe that this is all real, even now. But then, what is real? The most real things cannot be seen. When my children were young and growing into themselves, I used to think about who I was as a mother. I always believed in my heart that I was my children's hope. I was a positive force in their lives, believing in them, always thinking the best of them and for them. I trusted that their choices would eventually lead them to a positive place, a place of happiness. As a teacher, I believed I was my students' hope. No matter what the situation or circumstance, I held the sacred vessel of hope for each one of the children in my life. I still do. But now, I have traded my hope for my daughter Vicki for the blessed knowledge that all is well with her—she has shed her body, and she has transformed. *She is everything, for she is pure light. She is love.*

Yes, I can go to those places and feel a deep sorrow, a loss beyond all words, but my choice is to go on with creation instead of looking backward. I can look backward and smile with the memories, and I can look backward and learn, but I cannot live in the past. Memories are behind us, and we can visit them whenever we choose, but to live in those memories wastes the time we have to create now. We have come to this place called earth to *live*, and living is a forward movement. Yes, our loved one is part of our past and that can never change, but our loved one can be included in our forward movement with us if we choose to recognize them. I choose to include Vicki in my now! *When we see that the light energy of our loved one is alive, we can make that energy a part of today and allow it to enhance all that we do, creating new memories, our memories of tomorrow.*

Memories are living movies that our energy has created and can still create. *Memories are alive!* Our memories can never be destroyed, for they are a part of our energy's vibration. Consider this. Our loved one is spirit energy without a body—we, too, are spirit energy, but we have a body! Although our loved one's body has disappeared, the energy that he or she is, never ceases to be. When we remember people, we invite their energy into our movie, and indeed, they are there with us, part of our creation. When you remember some moment or time or feeling connected with your loved one, you are communing with that person. *It is really happening on some level!* It is also possible that sometimes the things we choose to remember are actually being shown *to* us to help us discover something that we need to see or understand. Maybe it is not *our* energy that is summoning memories back to us, but the energy of our loved one who is presenting us with an opportunity to experience this feeling again so that we can somehow benefit from reliving it. *What a gift that is, if we choose to see it!*

Perhaps, in a way, I had been preparing myself for this moment all my life. As a child, I was drawn to the energy of the rocks that lined the road and I held a reverence for the brilliantly colored autumn leaves that withered as the winter approached. I remember trying to rescue as many leaves as I could from their fate by gathering them and stashing them inside. I could feel the peace of an untouched snowfall in our backyard and had insisted that my brothers and sister not disturb it. Encouraged by my mother, whose life remains a positive inspiration to me, I thought a lot about the stars and the vastness of the universe, seeking wisdom and understanding in the movements of all life. In the years that followed, I continued my pursuit of finding answers to life's unanswerable questions through many avenues—I read books on metaphysical subjects, took classes in yoga, and explored the teachings of the church. My understanding grew with each new discovery, and when Daniel was in Iraq, I began writing inspirational poems and stories. It amazes me now to think of how that writing would connect to the future separation I would be forced to experience from my daughter's passing. I had been challenged by Elizabeth's moving away from home for her last year of high school and then again for college. The challenge mounted as I saw my son join the service and ship off for two tours of duty in a war zone. Of course, Vicki's childhood flying adventures were also mental and emotional adjustments for me, as were her time away in college and her two years spent in the Peace Corps in an underdeveloped Eastern European country. Those separations were personal opportunities for me to work on "letting go." There were tough moments, and I thought I had coped quite well under each unique circumstance.

But experiencing this, the greatest loss of my life, was devastating until my awareness began growing, and I saw the connection that it had to my past writing and learning. Had part of me—my unconscious self—known all along that this was coming? It seemed impossible to think, but I found so much in my writing to make me look at that possibility. About a month before Vicki left, I had given some advice to a friend who had lost her sister and was having a difficult time moving on. I suggested that she could feel her sister's presence if she opened up to it. I had taken a class on ancient Indian wisdom in Utah five months before, and during the class, I had experienced some profound happenings that proved to me that communication was possible to achieve with our loved ones who have left this plane. I encouraged my friend to look for signs from her sister and wrote to her in a message, "*Move the grief out. The quieter you become, the easier it is for you to hear.*" I had jotted that down on a small piece of paper and placed it by my computer since I thought the words sounded pretty wise. I don't know where they came from; I just remember being impressed that they came from my head. Well, about a month later, as I frantically checked my computer the day after my daughter left the earth, I noticed the words that I had written only weeks before, sitting right there in plain view on my desk: *Move the grief out. The quieter you become, the easier it is for you to hear.* I read the quote, my soul listened, and somehow I began following my own advice. Was this a coincidence?

Years earlier when my son was preparing to deploy for Iraq, I wrote a poem to reconcile my emotions about the reality of his going into harm's way and of my having no control over what was to be. I asked myself how I could live with his leaving and with the possibility of losing him. Writing that poem brought me comfort because it made me look at things from a higher perspective. It addressed my feelings of helplessness and calmed my fears. It made me see that I must trust God in His decision for my son. No matter what was to happen, my son was safe in the arms of God. My heart was with every one of the young men and women who were over there serving our country—I felt like each one was my own child. It is difficult for those not a part of the military family to understand how close we can all feel. When the first casualties began to come during the war, I wanted other mothers and families to feel some relief from their losses, so I researched the addresses of all the casualties. I pored over each one, praying for them, and I sent a letter of thanks and a copy of the poem to each of their families. I did this until I could no longer continue because it was time for my son to deploy and my heart needed some rest. I stopped sending the letters and the poems, but I sent my prayers of hope for all of us instead. Little did I know that my poem would bring comfort to *my* soul when my own daughter would leave this world. *Had I written it years before for me?*

For My Soldier

Where are you my son, my child, my love,
Can I know where you are?
If I could mount the moon with the stars, maybe I could peer,
'Til I found you in my view
Then you'd feel so near.

But, I can't know just where you are, or what it is you must do,
So, I will leave it all to God who holds the answer true.
For you, my son, have a destiny that I cannot see,
And try as I may I cannot know what it is meant to be.

That is the work which you and God have so very carefully planned,
And I must wait and trust in that and truly understand.
Understand that Gods sees you, too, as His child,
And know that He protects you now, and no true harm will allow.

My dear son, I love you so, what can I do for you?
I will pray that God and His angels will in all ways watch over you.
Do you hear me whisper, Son, whisper in your ear,
How I love you dearly, and wish that you were near?

I must be strong and carry on 'til I can touch your face,
And gaze in your eyes, and see you smile, and feel your embrace.

Quite a few years ago when Vicki was going through an exceptionally rough time in her life, I wrote a poem for her. It was my prayer. I could see her struggling, I knew she was hurting, and I wanted to do something to help her. Reading that prayer now, I am struck by its poignancy. Although I wrote it years before, *it seems it was meant just for her on that day she chose to leave.* My prayer appears to have been answered. Is that just a coincidence?

A Mother's Prayer for Her Daughter

Angels, carry her away for her soul to renew,
Relieve, restore, guide her,
May God's love make her new.
Let her find the road ahead that leads to happiness,
Let her heart and mind be free
To feel life's sweet caress.
Let her know how much she's loved in every way,
And strength receive from God above
Every single day.
May she trade the darkness for the beautiful light she is,
And may her soul breathe clean again,
Her precious gifts to give.

So many of my writings now had deeper meanings for me. Had they been created as a preparation of some sort, a preparation of me? It seemed so clear, right in front of my eyes. Could I really believe it? I could see that Vicki was connecting the dots for me now, revealing truths that I had struggled to see in my previous years of searching. Then I had only glimpsed the truth, but now it all came together for me in a way that I truly *knew* it and could now witness to those around me. I had the opportunity to help my family to higher understanding, and I now hope to do that for many others.

Victoria has continued to help make connections for me in the many weeks since she has gone. I have come to depend on her help, and I know she is pleased to give it to me. *This has led me to know that there is purpose in all that happens.* I have often heard that there are no accidents, and my experiences are showing me that, indeed, it is true. It is no accident that this book is in your hands right now. Life has a plan, and synchronicity reminds us of it, if we choose to embrace it. Synchronicity…a kind of divine perfection that reveals itself to us in the way life's seemingly ordinary happenings fit together in a pattern that shows us that something higher has dominion over this existence. Everything, great or small, happens for a purpose. *Everyone is connected and the movements of life are like a beautiful symphony, should we choose to open our ears and hear!* It is all a part of the order of the universe. Life…what a miracle! We may not understand how it all works together, but when we truly embrace these concepts with faith, our path is made clearer and easier to walk, for we can then see in the light that guides us along the way. *In that light, we need not fear; we need not suffer.*

My silence has helped me hear.

—Corinne Van Meter

The Messages Continue to Come

Our new relationship with Vicki has only blossomed through the weeks and months that have passed. Our lives continue to be peppered with her presence, sometimes in small seemingly insignificant ways and other times in incredible happenings that can't be denied! Each remembrance brings an added sense of peace to our souls. She continues to speak to each of us in ways that only *we* can understand, with words that only *we* can hear. I share some of these moments with you to let you see how imperceptibly the light of our loved ones can enter our lives, and *if we aren't paying attention, we could very well miss them!*

It was time to invite our extended family into the healing process. They had patiently waited until we were ready to have a gathering. Words cannot express the appreciation that I have for my four brothers and sisters, their spouses and all of Vicki's cousins and their spouses who loved us through our pain. They, too, had loved Vicki and it was difficult for them as well. I thank them not only for supporting us but also for understanding that we needed our time together to sort it all out. We are indeed blessed to feel such a strong bond of love and understanding for each other. What a gift to experience in this lifetime!

They planned a special memorial celebration of Vicki's life to take place in a central location, in Cleveland, where family from all over the country could meet. It made sense to have the event at the same place we had gathered the previous summer for a wedding shower for one of the fifteen cousins. Vicki, or Victoria as she had asked to be called in her later years, had been able to attend as she was freshly returned from her service in the Peace Corps. During the shower the previous year, Vicki, ever a baseball fan, sneaked into a bathroom, changed into her jeans, and met her boy cousins at the ball field to catch a game. May I add that it was the same park she had been invited to years ago to throw the first pitch for a game after her flight across the ocean. That was a real highlight for her!

At the hotel, we had a beautiful afternoon filled with laughter and tears sharing memories of Vicki's life. Her cousins prepared a slide presentation of lots of the happy times they had all spent together. All of the relatives, young and old, had an opportunity to speak. The room was filled with love. We celebrated Vicki and what she taught us, but before the afternoon ended, we all took a walk across the street to the ballpark where we watched a game together, with Vicki in our hearts and our minds. *She was there.* The home team won in an exciting game, breaking the tie in the bottom of the ninth! On the giant lighted screen above the fans flashed a person holding a sign of *VICTORY!* We all exchanged knowing glances as the name of the player who hit the winning run was emblazoned on the monitor before us. *His name... Victor Martinez!* We heard you, Vicki!

My husband, Jim, has struggled greatly with the loss of the physical presence of his daughter. He shared so many of the same traits with her and felt a bond because of it. He has had some incredible happenings occur in his life since Vicki left. He spent many days looking through the garage and the attic trying to find some kind of tangible message from her. He had heard her in his thoughts for so long and was greatly comforted by that, but as is the case with us humans, he wanted more. So, he searched until he found a single piece of paper in one of Vicki's old desks. That was odd because I had collected all of my children's school papers and had saved them in a separate place. What he found was a story that she had written for school, obviously one about her vacation. We had vacationed in the Bahamas when Vicki was in second grade. It was a fabulous trip for our family. We stayed in a tree house right next to an endless, white sand beach. The children were thrilled to experience this piece of nature! The first morning, Jim and I awoke to an empty house! Panicked, I ran to the window, flung the curtain open, and looked to the shore, where I spied my three exhilaratingly happy children splashing in the aquamarine waters along pure, white sand that went on for eternity. There was no one else in sight. I shall always treasure that picture. It was a wonderful time for us. Elizabeth, Daniel, and Vicki all got a chance to swim with the dolphins on that trip, a memory never to be forgotten. Jim vowed to build one of those tree houses one day. In fact, he later made contact with the company that produced them, and as the children grew, he never abandoned his plans to create one. He had imagined it would be for Vicki.

So, finding the story was bittersweet. He was happy to have found it because it made him remember the unforgettable time we all had, but he also felt sadness that he had not been able to fulfill his personal promise of building that very special building for his daughter. Well, later on that day, Jim received a telephone call. It was from the company he had contacted years before about building the tree house. Amazed, Jim started to explain to a man with whom he had never before spoken, why his plans had changed. The kind, seemingly angelic man said, "*You don't have to say anything else. I understand. I don't even know why I called you now. This note is seven years old.*" Jim was touched by his kind and gentle words and went to bed with the thought of contacting Vicki that night to let her know what had happened.

Thought dialogue began between them as it had so many nights before. She was helping her father adjust to her transformation into another existence. He asked if she had known that he wanted to build the tree house for her. They had never openly discussed it before. She immediately answered, "*Dad, why do you think the man called you today?*" Jim was, as he described it, so "giddy" with happiness at this connection that he wanted to wake me up and tell me immediately. Vicki cautioned him not to and told him, "*Don't, Dad, she's sleeping now.*" It would be like her to want me to sleep, something that she had difficulty doing for years. He eventually fell asleep and woke up euphoric!

This past summer, we attended our niece's wedding in Minnesota and decided, because we drove there, to continue on to visit the Dakotas and some of the parks in the area. Actually, it was going to be a memory tour. Eighteen years before, when Elizabeth and I attended a national speech competition in Fargo, North Dakota, Jim had made a similar trip with the two younger children, taking them to see the Badlands, Mr. Rushmore, Custer State Park, and Theodore Roosevelt National Park. He wanted me to see where they all had been and enjoyed such a memorable time. He planned to re-create for me the horseback ride that they had taken in Custer State Park. The ride had been a fabulous experience for them. I could see it in a classic family picture taken on the trip. We had it enlarged and had admired it for years. The kids are on horseback and visible only from the back, and the horses are dipping their heads down to drink from a stream lined with blowing grass. The picture turned out to look like a Monet painting when it was enlarged. It remains a treasure. Jim and I mounted our horses that morning, and to our surprise we turned out to be the first two in a line of about twenty young riders. It was the first time in our riding history that we ever had the privilege of being right behind the guide on a ride, and we were pleased because it afforded us some privacy during our nostalgic trip. While we rode through the rolling valleys under the steep, black hills and over the streams, we thought of Vicki. The grasses bent, and the birds played tag among the flowers and trees. Suddenly, Jim's cell phone rang, a surprise as there was no certain cell phone service in that part of the park. It was Vicki's first flight instructor, Bob! He lives in Florida, and we had not talked with him for some time. He wanted to know when Vicki's memorial service would be. *Little did he know that we were on one right then, and he was part of it.*

On our way back east, after our trip, we decided to spend some extra time in Iowa, Vicki's favorite state. We never knew why she liked it so much. Perhaps, it was because there is a town in Iowa called Van Meter. She had stopped there once on one of her trips traveling by herself across the United States to Utah and had even met someone who gave her a hat and a shirt from the town's fire department. We chose the town of Davenport in which to stop and browse. As we sat in a small German pub and ate lunch, I heard her tell me that I should walk down the street and look around because there was something there for me. I listened, and Jim and I started out on a walk. I didn't know what I was trying to find. Maybe it was in the old bookstore. No, we passed it by. I am interested in stones and jewelry making, so the window of the jewelry store caught my eye. There was a display of unusual stones there and as I studied it, I noticed a smaller display to my left. It was a beautiful necklace with a symbol dangling from it. I had never seen anything like it before. *My jaw dropped in astonishment, and I felt my heart beating inside my chest!* The contemporary piece in front of my eyes was called "Mother and Child," and it was the shape of two connecting circles representing *the unity of mother and child from birth to infinity!* I smiled and softly wept. I had listened, and I had found my gift from Vicki.

I believe that when we acknowledge that these happenings are not coincidences, but instead are *real* contacts from the energy of our loved ones, when we recognize them, they come through to us more and more, stronger and stronger, louder and clearer. I am always thanking Vicki, letting her know that I believe. I know that she is trying to work through me here, and I am grateful. Just the other day I asked her advice: "Vicki, what do you think?" She shot back the thought, *"Mom, I don't need to think; I feel!"* We have a running dialogue when I pay attention. I am blessed for this awareness. I recently attended a silent retreat, and while there, I strengthened my connection to myself, to that part of me that is part of all. Vicki is there. So are all those who have gone before us, there just waiting to be recognized. Since my time at the retreat, I have begun writing again. My silence has helped me hear.

At that retreat center, Jim stayed with me for one night before the retreat officially began. There were beautiful, quiet woods on the property with gardens and trails where a person could commune with nature. Jim and I followed a shaded path among the towering trees that were dappled with golden specks of sunlight. We slowly walked along, Jim in front of me. I had fallen behind a bit when I noticed that Jim turned very suddenly and looked behind him; then he felt the top of his head. He stopped and turned to me with an unbelieving look on his face. Something or someone had actually touched his head. The pressure was unmistakable. He had been walking in contemplation, thinking of Vicki. Of course, nothing we could see with our eyes had touched his head. I was walking right behind him the whole time. Jim had been touched from another dimension. He had never before experienced anything like that, and he was in awe.

One day, when I was straightening up some odds and ends near the door to our attic in the upstairs hallway, I lifted up a wreath from a table that had nothing else on it, and I found a picture. That's odd...I did not recognize anything about it. Why would I keep this unknown picture, let alone find it in such an unusual place and on that day? I looked closer. There were tables in the picture with people sitting at them facing a stage. I looked still closer and noticed a character in costume on the platform...it was either Mickey or Minnie. That was it: Disney World! I had gone there once by myself with Vicki. It was from our first night together at the park. This night began her experience in that magical world. She was thrilled being there, and I was delighted to be experiencing it with her. Actually, it was not her first time at Disney World. We had dragged her there once before on a family trip. I say dragged because that's what we did to her. She was mesmerized, and the wonder of it all had stunned her, and we, as a family of four, older, seasoned visitors barreled our way past all the delights of a first timer. Jim and I had decided that I would take her back so she could really enjoy it at a friendly pace, and that's what we did. She loved everything, especially Epcot. At that time, her favorite characters were Chip and Dale. The day we arrived, we took the monorail to the Contemporary Resort Hotel and bought her two favorite stuffed animals in the gift shop. Chip and Dale accompanied us to the Hawaiian luau later at The Polynesian Resort where we stayed on this trip. The picture I held had been taken that night at the luau. That was the back of my head as I looked up at the stage. *Vicki had taken that picture!* It was a magical night there with my little girl. And this was a magical moment now. Vicki wanted me to remember that wondrous time. If I had not been aware, I could have tossed the picture out without thinking and missed the lovely memory that it had given me. I thanked Vicki for my gift.

Last week, I traveled to a neighboring city to help my sister set up her classroom for the start of the school year. I had volunteered to help organize and make bulletin boards for her. It would be a two-day trip. I packed my little bag and readied myself for the journey. I decided to wear old clothing, as the building was undergoing lots of construction and I had been warned that conditions were pretty much a mess. I chose to wear the silver bracelet, ring, and earrings that I had painstakingly made from scratch at a silversmithing class I had taken. I was proud of my work and wanted to spruce up my drab look. As I put on one of the earrings, a little voice somewhere said, "You'll lose one of these." I didn't listen, and I hopped into the car wearing my silver jewelry and headed for my sister's house.

She and I arrived at the school, a career center where she trains future nurses, and I got right to work. She was right; the place was pretty much a mess. My sister and one of her nieces were working unpacking boxes and organizing things, and I set to work doing the same. I went through boxes and boxes of linens and books and papers, throwing much away, organizing the rest. Scattered around the room were barrels of junk to be discarded, and empty boxes lined the hallway. I made hospital beds, dressed mannequins, and hopped all over the place. I put my hand to my ear and noticed that one of my earrings was gone. My first reaction was to be a bit panicked just because that earring had taken so long to make. I scurried around looking for it but realized that it was pretty much like finding a needle in a haystack. I remembered the little voice and figured that I had been warned, but then I told myself that I would cool it and do what I had come to do and that was to help my sister. I would have some consultation with Vicki later that night after checking around in my car and at my sister's home.

I went to bed with the question of the earring in my mind, but I didn't seem to get an answer from Vicki until I opened my eyes the next morning and a voice inside my head said, *"You will find it. Look very closely."* I couldn't stop thinking about a particular barrel in the room. I imagined that the earring was in something white with black on it. Resolving that people were more important than things and that I would make another earring sometime, I calmly went back to school with my sister to complete another day's work, but decided I'd at least *look closely* for the rest of the day. I arrived at the room and walked straight to the barrel that had been in my mind's eye. I used a paper towel to pull out all the discarded junk, shaking it all as I did. Nothing. *Look closely.* There was an old Styrofoam coffee cup, some dirt, and an unidentifiable liquid filling the bottom of the barrel. I also saw a white crumpled piece of cloth. *Look closely.* The voice made me refuse to stop. I picked up the floating objects, and, to my amazement, *I found my earring gleaming up at me from the middle of the soupy mix!* We all stood there in disbelief. I'm so glad I listened. I'm so glad I trusted what I heard. Finding that earring became more proof to me that I had received real messages. Thank you, Vicki.

One night, Vicki's cousin had a dream about her. She contacted me immediately to tell me about it because it had been so real to her. Vicki and she were walking in the mall together holding hands. Now, walking in the mall holding her cousin's hand would not have been something she would have done here on earth. They were walking and talking, and her cousin said, "Vicki, this is all so hard to believe. Aren't you supposed to be gone? I just can't believe it!" Vicki answered, *"The reason you can't believe it is because I'm still here."* Perhaps her cousin can move through the times of her life knowing that Vicki's hand is always close, ready to share love, and to give comfort and direction in time of need. Perhaps, Vicki wanted to let her know that they are always connected.

One of her closest friends from childhood reported a similar dream. In that dream, the two walked through the streets of our old hometown just like they had done years ago. They shared a spirited and mischievous sense of humor, and they always created fun together. This dream was no exception. Vicki kept hiding from people as they wound through the streets of town, and she was laughing. Her friend heard her say that she was hiding because she wasn't supposed to show herself. Her friend woke up not being able to distinguish the dream from reality. Which experience was real? Is it possible that *we* are the ones who are living in a dream?

Both Elizabeth and Daniel continue to have contact with their sister. Those contacts have come into their lives at times and in ways that are meaningful just to them. Elizabeth had been asking many questions about Vicki's choice to leave this life. She couldn't understand why, and it plagued her. She was wrestling with these unknowns when she received an invitation from someone she barely knew from an acting class, someone who invited her to go to a movie. Her classmate had admired the director of this movie, and he asked Elizabeth to come with him to see it even though neither of them knew what it was about.

Ordinarily, she would not have accepted the invitation and, instead, would have declined because of her own sadness, but for some reason, she found herself at the theater. The movie began, and she realized that it was about a man who had lost a friend in the same way Elizabeth had just lost her sister. Stunned, she didn't know if she could handle watching any more of a movie that so closely resembled her life, but instead of leaving, something made her stay to see if there was a message in it for her.

Now, Vicki was a movie buff. She even assisted with the shooting of one of Elizabeth's movies and thought that she might want to pursue movie production for a vocation. Vicki eventually changed her mind, but she and her sister remained connected through this shared interest.

So, Elizabeth continued to watch the movie with her new friend. It was almost as if Vicki was talking to her on the screen that night. There were close-ups, full-screen images of the face of the girl who took her own life, and she stared into Elizabeth's eyes. She explained that she had followed her *own* life journey and that hers was different than that of her friend's. *Now it was up to the man to follow his own path in life.* By being present with the movie, Elizabeth was receiving answers to many of the questions with which she had been wrestling, and she felt as if the actor's words were meant just for her. *She felt Vicki speaking to her!* But she was astonished when she saw nuns skydiving. Of course, Vicki was a pilot, *but she was also a skydiver!* Elizabeth left the theater in shock, as did her new friend. They walked along and talked, and she discovered that her friend's mother had been born in Moldova where Vicki had been stationed during her time in the Peace Corps and that her friend was born on her grandmother's birthday, someone who had been especially close to Elizabeth throughout her life. All coincidences?

After Vicki left, Daniel had a difficult time adjusting to all that he was required to do at school. He was especially close to her, and the tragedy hit him hard. He was also dealing with the adjustment to civilian life when it all happened. Still, he had to move on in his studies to complete his first semester back in school after many years away from the pressures of college work. One evening, he tried to get away to find some quiet place to think. He found himself in a small, out-of-the-way bar that he had once visited. Thinking that it would be as quiet as he had remembered, he was surprised to see it practically full and noisy when he arrived, but he found a seat open at the end of the bar and decided to stay for a while. He sat there for about a half an hour next to a man who said nothing, and then he heard him mutter something about having a bad day. Daniel knew what a bad day was, so he engaged the stranger in conversation, thinking that he could be of comfort to him. The man shared some of his story. He was a very accomplished teacher—a teacher of actors, and he had come to this country from Denmark a number of years ago. His work had taken him all over the world from Denmark to

Russia to Bali. He worked with his students using masks, and one of the classes he taught was about combating fear. This interested Daniel, and he listened. Perhaps this man had a message. Daniel began opening up, sharing his feelings about what he had gone through in the past month with the loss of Vicki. The man continued to explain that his specialty was mask therapy, and he invited Daniel to take part in a class. They had a long conversation together, and before he left, he turned to Daniel and said, "*You know, I didn't know why I chose this place to come tonight, but I know now.*" We never know where help is going to come from. I believe Vicki knew what her brother needed. Daniel eventually went to a session with this teacher, and he was helped in his healing process.

Our friend and neighbor, who was one of the kind people who had helped us at the time of Vicki's passing, is a contributor to our local newspaper. She had graciously chosen to write an article to honor our daughter whose accomplishments had brought pride to the small town where we lived. To prepare for her article, she read some of the memorabilia we had saved from Vicki's flying days. One of those special documents was a letter of congratulations from President Bill Clinton. She read this letter with special interest as she is an avid fan of the former president. It just so happened that within days of her reading the letter, Bill Clinton made an appearance at a college in our town where he was doing some campaigning for his wife. Our neighbor attended. She was in awe and amazement to get so close to the former president, her hero, and when the speech was concluded, she was thrilled to shake his hand. After the greeting, Mr. Clinton walked quite a distance past her and began talking with someone when the thought came into her mind: *tell him about, Vicki.* Immediately after receiving that message, immediately after that feeling came over her, *Bill Clinton turned and walked straight back toward her, stopped in front of her, and gazed straight into her eyes and waited to hear what she had to say!* She asked if he remembered the little girl who flew the airplane across the country when he was president. He responded that, of course, he remembered her. She told him what had just recently happened to Vicki, and the president was noticeably stunned and deeply saddened. As he compassionately patted his heart and shook his head from side to side in what she described as true pain, our friend experienced several moments of heart connection with a former president of the United States. It was a memory of a lifetime for her. They were brought together by Vicki's message. Vicki had known just how much this experience would mean to her neighbor and friend. Another incredible gift.

I tell you these things to let you know how close we are to those we love who have gone home. *They are as close as a thought.* I tell you these things so that you, too, can see them living in your life, so that you might look for them with open eyes, open ears, open heart, open mind. I tell you these things so that you might welcome into your life the love they are still trying to share with you. They are still present, helping in ways that cannot be fully comprehended. I tell you these things to bring you peace.

I choose with every breath. What do I choose?

—Corinne Van Meter

Vicki's Message to Me

One night shortly after Vicki left, I received a clear message. The next morning, my head was full of words. Those words, I believed, held some special meaning, and I wanted to share them with others, so I made sure to include them in a diary I started to remember the messages I was receiving from Vicki. I know now that those words were meant for *me*. Maybe they came from Vicki, maybe she completed a circle of contact for me with a higher understanding, I do not know. What I do know is that they have remained in my mind and in my heart, and I am reminded of them as I travel this journey that I am now living, this journey that I have grown to know as a magical expansion into an infinite world far beyond this reality that we have all created. I offer those words to you.

How to Live

Be kind... in ways large and small to everyone and everything.
Listen... to the soft voice inside that speaks your truth.
Talk.... with God.
Learn... about who you are.
Laugh... share the light with the world.
Enjoy... drink in love.
Live... with heart.
Just a vacation this time on earth, just a moment on a magical journey!

Everyone is special, and Vicki would be the first one to remind us all of that fact. She never thought that she was better than anyone else. I can honestly say that Victoria's life here and beyond has shown her to be extraordinary. Not only was she able to connect with so many through her youthful accomplishments during her life here on earth, but she was also able to make solid connections, both quickly and strongly, shortly after passing into the next existence. Perhaps she came to show us something. We all do that for each other in lots of ways, great and small, but some individuals seem to affect the masses of people while they are here on earth. I believe Vicki in her humble, unpretentious way was one of those people.

I am left to wonder what my part was in her mission. She has told me many times in thought, *"You were my words when I could not speak."* I used to help her formulate her speeches when she was younger, and on many occasions, I was the one to jump-start her thinking if she was stuck when writing school papers. Now I realize that I was her voice in the many moments when she could not speak for herself during her years of personal struggle. I had tried to understand her through it all. Perhaps, some of my writings somehow came from a part of her that she could no longer express. And, perhaps my writing now is coming from that same place. I do not know.

She knew about some of the stories that I had written and of my desire to publish them. During her last trip to North Carolina, I shared a recording that I had made of an inspirational children's book that I had written. I did this while she was in Moldova during her time in the Peace Corps. I remember that she quieted herself and really listened to it, and then sat there and just smiled. Ordinarily, she would have poked fun at me, but this time she didn't. Perhaps, Vicki/Victoria, that amazing soul that came to this earth through me, somehow knew that she would eventually be helping me achieve my purpose of helping others to know who they really are. I am so grateful that I lived in the moment enough to remember those feelings and to be able to recall so many other things that she has said.

I have been recalling words that my daughter has spoken through the years, words that give me pause and words that, in their remembrance, remain a precious gift. I think remembering words spoken by our loved ones in poignant moments of our lives is very precious. When Vicki was only three, I recall an incident that happened at the local department store where we went to buy some new blue jeans. Frills and ruffles were the newest fashion, and on Vicki's tiny frame, I thought jeans adorned in such a feminine way would be very becoming. Of course, my baseball-lovin', classic-tasted little girl loved the basic, plain, old, regular straight-legged blue jeans. We went into the dressing room, and she tried on both kinds. I *oohed* and *aahed* at the fancy ones while she ignored my display of approval. But when she slipped on her favorites, she smiled at her reflection in the mirror. I admit that it was one of those moments when I tried to manipulate her into doing my bidding. I reviewed her choices throwing in the fact that she looked "just darling" in the pretty jeans. I then asked my carefully posed question: "Which ones should we get?" Naturally, she answered by pointing to her favorites. With an adult pout, I added, "Well, maybe we should come back another day." She wisely turned to me and calmly replied, "Mother, whose choice is it?" I got the picture. Her words went straight to my soul. "*Mother, whose choice is it?*" Choices. She taught me so much that day, and I can never forget that moment. She continues to teach me through those words now as I read an even deeper meaning into that message. She was and still is speaking to my soul. Back then, her words gave me the opportunity to be wise. Now, I think they are meant to bring comfort to my heart. Treasure words, but remember—to hear the words, you must listen, and to listen, you must be present. Here. Now. *In the moment.*

What we spend our time doing here matters. It becomes an integral part of the whole of who we are, of who we all are together. It has its affect on everything and everyone. Over ten years ago, I wrote a poem for the at-risk students whom I taught. I had gone back to teaching after Vicki's flights and decided that I needed to share what I had learned through the experiences of raising my own children. I had learned so much, and I desperately wanted all children to know how powerful and capable they are, how full of light and possibility each one is. I sat in my classroom before the first day of school trying to put into words a simple message for them to understand.

ME

What I say matters
What I do matters
What I think matters
What I feel matters
WHO I AM MATTERS
The world needs me.

It was posted at the front of my classroom for the years that I taught and became our mantra for all the classes that passed through my door. *WHO I AM MATTERS! ALWAYS! ALL THROUGH MY LIFE!* My choices matter in this world. They determine quality of life for me and for those around me. I can choose to bring pain and sadness to myself and others, or I can choose to bring life, forgiveness, understanding, and joy as my contributions to humanity. *I choose with every breath. What do I choose?*

I believe that Victoria now understands and knows the fullness of human potential and that she wants all to experience that potential while they are still on the earthly plane. I also believe that she is encouraging me to relate to others what I have learned through the experience of sharing her life. For as closed as she became on this plane, she has now opened up, allowing her gifts of love to pour out upon the earth. I know that my daughter's sacrifice has brought me to a new place of understanding. She has taught me how to live each day. One of her cousins spoke that truth at Vicki's Celebration of Life when she said, "Vicki gave us the gift of life. *She gave her life so we could really live.*" I believe that. This writing is part of that gift, and all that I do after this moment shall be also. I move forward in my life with my daughter as close to me as she can possibly be. She touches my face gently with her kiss; she whispers softly into my ear; she lives in the thoughts of my mind. I shall always listen, I shall always feel her presence, and I will live in the love that she is. I celebrate her, and I smile.

There is no time; there is no space. This love you feel can't be erased.

—Corinne Van Meter

A New Life Begins

Vicki shared with me some time ago that although she is busy with her existence in the new world where she is, she will always be near us. She has vowed not to leave us again as long as we are in this world. I believe that. I believe that whatever we do, wherever we are, she will be there—present, helping to guide us along the way. We need only think of her. We need only listen. Our lives will forever be rich with you, our beloved Vicki, for your divine inspiration will be alive in the work that we do on this earth whatever that may be.

Jim wants to do more volunteer work out in nature, and he intends to be involved in projects that offer Vicki's life as inspiration for others. I think Vicki will approve. For now, Elizabeth will use the gift of laughter in her work to lighten the burdens of the world. Vicki will love that. At this time, Daniel plans to gain knowledge so that he can assist others in reaching their potentials. Vicki will be proud of that. I intend to do my best to help heal the world of needless suffering. I know Vicki expects that of me. For to whom much has been given, much is expected. I have received so very much from knowing you, my amazing daughter. You and I are one, and we will work together for good.

I no longer believe, I know. And my knowing has changed the way I live this life. I have grown to know that the beauty of the new fallen snow is not destroyed by a footprint, and the leaves on the trees wither only for a moment. Snow comes again. Buds return. All of life lives on. And so it is . . .

✣

What magic we are living in, and we don't even realize it!

—Corinne Van Meter

My Hope for You

Look at your grief; honor it, but look past its presence in your life. It is not all of you, but only part of your experience here on earth. Realize that *you* are greater than it! Connect with the inner light that you are. In that light, you will feel your loved one, for your loved one is part of that light in you. We cannot live on this earth without facing loss. It's part of the experience of being on earth. We lose loved ones, pets, jobs, relationships, dreams. Yes, each loss is challenging to overcome, but all loss is actually opportunity, opportunity to look deeper into ourselves to find that connection with something more than our earthly self. If we choose to look inward, we will find a healing light that has no end: a light that, in its brightness, brings a profound peace and immeasurable joy; a light that can change our world. Keep the channel open to that light which burns inside of you. How do we do that?

Keeping the channel open takes constant effort. It requires living in the now, or recognizing each moment. Get in touch with your inner self by relaxing, meditating, connecting to your thoughts and feelings by being silent enough to notice them. Some people can quiet their thoughts while exercising. Spending time in nature can make it happen, too. So can just walking at a slow pace and noticing the sights, sounds, and feelings of the elements. The simple act of breathing is an automatic connection to spirit. Just recognizing the breath is a wonderful way to relax. Many books have been written on the subject. A yoga class can teach you how to do it and help you practice. Surrounding yourself with relaxing stimuli is important—fresh flowers, soothing music, falling water, green plants, stones, and crystals—whatever brings a sense of serenity and peace to your life. As you begin opening up and discovering things, journaling your internal dialogue will help you get in touch with a whole new world. When you keep a record of your thoughts, memories, signs, and dreams, you can go back and remind yourself of what has been revealed to you. Help yourself get past the physical body to feel the light body that you are. It will allow an opportunity for the light of your loved one to communicate with you. It will allow an opportunity for you to transcend the challenging events in your life and bring you that peace which you seek. Please record all the treasure that you find. The gifts awaiting you are beautiful and healing!

Make room for a new way to touch the light which is your loved one. You will find the most extraordinary things happening! Only you will know their whispers for they are meant only for you to hear and understand. Look past your grief, and make yourself an open channel at this most precious time—a time when the veil is so thin. Your loved one is so close, trying to reach you to show you the gift of life that is still there. The love that is, was, and forever shall be—for you and for them. *What magic we are living in, and we don't even realize it!*

Just yesterday, I received a phone call from one of my sisters. In the late spring, she had planted the flower bulbs that were given to family members in Vicki's memory when we had been all together back in April. She had watched the flowerless shoots springing up from the earth all summer long, and it was now the beginning of fall. On this day, she made her rounds of the yard and noticed one single, astonishingly beautiful, fuchsia and pale, golden-yellow bloom. It touched her heart, and she knew it was a message from Vicki—a sign to her that Vicki's light still shines on the earth.

Your new connection begins with the rebirth of your loved one into a new life, one that is more magical than we can fathom. We are permitted to glimpse this new life when we allow ourselves to be open to receiving, and in doing so, we, too, are reborn. So many little things, so many moments that in the past I would have considered coincidence, I now know they are not. They are the synchronicity of all life expressing itself! Intricate patterns are connecting, mysteriously weaving themselves together to create a beautiful picture. Open up, let all of life into your being! Miracles—like luscious fruit—are waiting to be plucked and eaten and savored. Delight in the gifts of the spirit that will come to you! You will experience closeness with your loved one that you have never known—a deep, joyous, ever-changing relationship. When you recognize your loved one, you honor that person. What a comforting, healing thing that is for both of you, and what a gift it becomes for all of life! Maybe someday, we body lights will knowingly work in concert with the lights of heaven. What miracles we could create together!

I have grown to know that the beautiful light that *was* my daughter still *is* that beautiful light, only it is even more magnificent! She has become part of the brilliance of God, an energy that can never be destroyed. It is my hope that the part of you that is your soul has listened, truly heard my story, and has recognized the truth in its message. I want the love that is your lost loved one to be found in the light of your heart, and I pray for you to know it and to walk in peace with that love in the dawning of the rest of your days.

Love & Light,

Corinne

Light a Candle for Me

Do not grieve my passing; I have come to you,
Because there are some things I would like for you to do.
Your soul knows I am safe, safe in the light—
The love you feel, the love I am holds me tight.

Do not worry about me—I am not alone,
I have other lights here, I am merely Home.
I have all I want in this wonderful light—
I need nothing, I am all right.

What I can use, you can still do for me.
Would you try; will you light a candle for me?
It's a different kind of candle, not like the ones you know.
This candle's light is quite unique—it gives a special glow.

Its light begins in your heart and spreads and spreads and grows,
Until it fills your being with a wondrous glow!
It will make you smile; it will make you sing,
It will let you play, and joy to others bring!

Soon the light will spread to everyone around,
And I will see its glow from high above the ground.
Will you do that, do that for me?
Send the sparkling light of love for me to see?

Light heart candles for me, light heart candles in the life below
So I can see their brilliance. How many hearts can you make glow?
We can see the glow of love, yes, it is so...
That glow makes us complete—we use it to grow.

When you see a sunset from a beach on earth,
A rainbow-colored sunset, it's a sight of precious worth.
It's like that here at Home…we see sunsets, too.
When we look back to earth, the sunsets are in you.

The animals are glowing, so are the plants and the trees,
And the insects, and the fish that swim in the seas.
We want to see people's love burn inside of them, too.
Could you light the spark of love so they glow just like you?

Another thing I ask of you, another thing to do—
This one is so simple—please listen when I talk to you.
Look for signs I will give to you—some will be so small
A little feather, some words, perhaps, maybe a call.

Maybe I'll come to visit you in the flicker of a light
Or in the twinkling of the stars you gaze into at night.
Maybe in a dream I will come, maybe a touch you will feel,
Make no mistake—I'm there—it is very real!

One more thing before I go, one more thing to do…
Laugh for me, please laugh for me, I want you to.
A laugh to us is a special light; it's wonderful and bright,
It's like a comet sent straight from earth…Spirit's delight!

The light it brings, the peace it makes you will never know.
Trust me, laugh for me…it will touch my soul!
I must go, but look for me; I'm always so near—
Walking with you, feeling your heart, shed not a tear.

I will wait in the light until I see you there,
Until then, fill your days with goodness and with care.
Until then, feel my love shining on you there,
Brighter than the biggest sun—a love all light can share!

It won't be long 'til you are Home—just you wait and see,
Just a blink—an eye's wink and you will be with me.
Make your life a gift of life, and give it back to me...
I will be rejoicing for all eternity!

Corinne & Victoria Van Meter
2008

Remember all the wondrous moments in such a special life.

Smile and feel the honor it was to experience this light!

—Corinne Van Meter

Epilogue

March 2009

Since my initial writings six months ago, I have been continually visited by Vicki's presence in many profound moments. She weaves in and out of my daily life and blesses me when I least expect it.

One of those moments took place in mid-December. Jim and I had made a short day trip to a city about thirty-five miles north of our home to do some Christmas shopping. We were planning a gathering with Elizabeth and Daniel in New York City, where they both now live. It would be our first Christmas since Vicki's passing. We knew it would be challenging. It was so hard to imagine being joyful without our entire family together at Christmas. It seemed that earthly matters, even celebrations, were not as important as they once used to be. Still, Jim and I wanted to make an effort to have some physical gifts to share with Elizabeth and Daniel. There still is family to celebrate, and we realized that we had to begin making new traditions in our family's life. So, we penned Vicki's two rambunctious dogs in the kitchen and hoped we would return before too much damage was done. After the outing, we made our way back home through the ice and snow and entered a cold, dark house. I rushed to the kitchen and saw blankets and bowls and dog beds scattered through the room, but as I scoured the area, I noticed something else…*on the floor in the midst of all the day's commotion was a perfectly shaped monarch butterfly with its wings frozen open!!!!* My mouth dropped, and I was incredulous: how could a perfect butterfly end up in our kitchen in freezing cold December? We supposed that Vicki was paying a Christmas visit to her beloved dogs, maybe keeping them company while we were away.

Then there was her appearance on Christmas Eve when we were in church for the evening candlelight service. Despite our mellow feelings, it was beautiful to hear the carols, smell the pine, see the lights. I was listening to the message being delivered from the pulpit when my eyes magically moved to the chrismon tree to the right. The tree was filled with the traditional pearly, iridescent white ornaments of religious symbols, and it glittered under the white lights that hugged its boughs. But my vision went straight to the one ornament that glowed into my eyes as brightly as the Star of Bethlehem. I moved from side to side and still, the brightness of the glare was blinding. I could hardly believe it, but then, the corners of my mouth rose into a smile that came from my very soul. My daughter was here with us. I nudged my family. They saw it, too. I was filled with the presence of Vicki. After the service, I made my way to the tree checking it out to see if it was a special ornament, one that lit up, perhaps. Maybe that was it? But, as I approached, I could see clearly that it was a simple shape covered in foil. The lights above had caught it the right way and sent its glimmer straight to where we sat. Nothing extraordinary some might reason, *except that it was in the shape of a butterfly!*

Then there was a message from her while we were on a family trip together in January. Jim and I had decided to create a memorable time for our two grown children by sharing with them some of the places we had traveled in recent years. We were waiting for a bus to take us back to our hotel after a day walking through the rainforest and on the beach at Manuel Antonio, Costa Rica. Relaxing until our bus arrived, Jim, Elizabeth, Daniel and I were perched on some concrete piers when we were approached by a vendor selling his wares. He was a young man holding some colorful homemade clay pots in his hand, and my children recognized him from meeting him earlier that day on the beach. He stopped to make some conversation with us. "Is this your family?" he asked. "Papa, Mamma, Sister, Brother…are there any others?" "No," we responded, shaking our heads and looking into each other's eyes. He asked once again, "Are there any more?" We once again replied that there were no others. Insisting, he asked still again, *"Are you sure?"* All at once I understood. I shook my head and explained that yes, there was one more, but she was—I pointed upward to the sky. Then to our amazement, this stranger in a foreign land smiled and delivered this message: "*Aaah, yes! She is free!*" Indeed, she *is* free.

And now it is one year since. Time to remember...I do believe that like our body, so too, our mind has a "muscle memory." As the calendar ticked away toward the anniversary date of Vicki's leaving, I began experiencing a deep foreboding. I found myself weeping for seemingly unknown reasons, having many moments of sadness creep into my days. It was as though I was unconsciously reliving the experience as if it had not yet happened. I was preparing for the trauma to come. I did not choose to do this; the experience seemed to have chosen me. Each one of us was having some anticipation anxiety.

We began making plans to be together during the week preceding the anniversary of our loss. We decided to spend that time out west in a community where our new permanent home would be located. From the back patio, we have a breathtaking view of distant mountains and red rocks. Vicki, in her earthly life, had visited the area and had been rejuvenated by hiking the canyons and cliffs that appear in the vast distances outside our new backyard window. In the seemingly insignificant conversation with Jim, she had made a request to have her ashes spread among the red rocks of southern Utah in the event should anything happen to her. We knew what we needed to do; we needed to release Vicki's ashes to their freedom in the beautiful resting place that she had chosen. Jim and I had explored the canyon months prior searching for the right resting spot. We found many possibilities on our trek—places that we knew Vicki had hiked and enjoyed, but we both seemed to sense what would become the final resting place. On the day that we found it, I sat on a giant rock overlooking a vast canyon, and I asked Vicki if this was the place. There was no answer from her, but as I stood up to leave, I heard a loud swishing in the silence and looked up to see a golden eagle fly over our heads. This was the place.

So, exactly one year from the date of Victoria's passing, we drove, pretty much in silence, to the canyon. We chose the end of the afternoon as our time. As we walked along the path toward our chosen spot, Daniel noticed a large bird circling in the distance in the cobalt blue sky above the red canyon rocks and wondered aloud if it was the eagle that had given its approval of Vicki's resting place. We reached the spot and looked out into a clear, blue sky toward an enormous rock in the distance, the sun still towering over it. We opened the green, satiny bag in which Vicki's ashes had rested for nearly a year to the moment and separated her ashes into four bags so that each of us could release some into the nooks and crannies, onto the aged pines, and over the rocks that lay around us. I had brought my Native American flute, and I felt inspired to sit on the rocks and play it from my heart for my daughter. Yes, for my daughter, but also for each one of us so that we could release ourselves too. I felt the sun on my face and closed my eyes. Sometimes I thought I could hardly breathe, but still I played. As I played, I watched as my husband and two children lovingly and peacefully blended our Vicki's physical presence with the beauty of the earth. They each paused to look my way, offering me serene smiles. We had been raised up. Family and friends were praying from afar, they were all there with us in spirit. It was awesome to experience.

Finally, it was my turn to release. I had been reluctant, but as I moved among the rocks sowing the ashes, I felt a sense of opening up and a joy in seeing that my daughter was becoming a part of everything that would keep on living until the end of time. I climbed to the top of the rock that looks out over the immense valley and flung ashes into the gentle breeze and as I did, two large birds flew over my head. One seemed to lead the other, and it flapped its wings freely and easily. The other followed, gliding in the sky behind. As we finished our ceremony, we looked up to the sky and noticed that the sun had retreated behind the massive rock that had been the backdrop for our experience, and we could see Vicki's resting spot in the cool, vibrant shade of the end of the day—a time she so dearly loved in the canyon. It seemed that all was well and that we and Vicki had come to a new sense of peace. This ceremony had been for Vicki, but it was for us, too. Now, we could both feel free to move on. Maybe that is what those two birds meant…we will both be moving forward together, Vicki is just in the lead. I thank God for bringing us to this place of understanding.

In the time since my daughter's passing a year ago, I have grown to heights that I could never have imagined. Sometimes, it is still so hard to believe. It feels like forever since she left her earthly life with us, and yet, it still feels like it happened only yesterday. I cannot and will never forget her laughter, her voice, her smile, her life, but I know that I must move past dwelling on those remembrances for I will hold us both back to live in a dream that is past, one that has its place in what has been. That dream always exists and can never be destroyed. I can visit it anytime with gladness in my heart, but now I am challenged to look forward and to live and create what will be my future in the time I have left here on this planet. She is here to help guide me along, yes, but I need to make my life happen for me. No one or nothing else can do that.

I know that the essence of my daughter is in a creation of its own now, somewhere beyond what I can see…in an existence that I cannot fully understand. But the beauty revealed to me is that I can always feel her presence by embracing this new place where she lives. I need only open my heart and use all of my senses to touch it, for it is there just waiting to be experienced. Vicki's love is all around me, mingling with the vibration of all creation now and for always.

Fly High My Love

You are the whisper of the wind,
You are the light that's in my eye,
You are the love within my heart,
Now you can fly…

You are the rain upon my cheek
When the skies speak out to me,
You are the warmth of the sun
That comforts me.

Fly high my love and fly free…
Now nothing in your way…
Be all that you can be…
Love always stays.

You are the mystery of the moon,
You are the wisdom in the stars,
You are the earth beneath my feet,
That's what you are.

You are the song of the bird,
The beauty of a day in spring,
Soft petals from a fragrant flower,
You're everything.

Fly high my love, and fly free…
Now nothing in your way…
Be all that you can be…
Love always stays.

So warm my face with your light,
Kiss the morning with the dew,
I'll feel the breeze run through my hair,
Knowing it's you…
I'll feel the breeze run through my hair,
Knowing it's you.

For Vicki
With love,
Mother
2009

Message
Journal

The quieter you become,
the easier it is to hear.

—Corinne Van Meter

❦

You are invited to share your story with the author at:

cev@CorinneVanMeter.com